SUPPORT OUR TROOPS

EASTER PARADE

EASTER PARADE

STEVE ENGLEHART

illustrated by
Adrienne Picchi

AN AVON CAMELOT BOOK

EASTER PARADE is an original publication of Avon Books. This work has never before appeared in book form.

AVON BOOKS
A division of
The Hearst Corporation
1350 Avenue of the Americas
New York, New York 10019

Copyright © 1995 by Steve Englehart
Cover art by Jane Chambless Wright
Interior text design by Kellan Peck
Illustrations copyright © 1995 by Adrienne Picchi
Published by arrangement with the author
Library of Congress Catalog Card Number: 94-31035
ISBN: 0-380-77417-8

Library of Congress Cataloging in Publication Data:
Englehart, Steve.
    Easter parade / Steve Englehart: illustrations by Adrienne Picchi.
        p.   cm.—(An Avon Camelot Book)
1. Easter—Juvenile literature. 2. Jesus Christ—Resurrection—Juvenile literature.
[1. Easter. 2. Jesus Christ—Resurrection.]
I. Title.
BV55.E54   1995   94-31035
394.2'667—dc20   CIP

First Avon Camelot Printing: March 1995

AVON TRADEMARK REG. U.S. PAT. OFF. AND IN OTHER COUNTRIES, MARCA REGISTRADA, HECHO EN U.S.A.

Printed in the U.S.A.

UNV 10 9 8 7 6 5 4 3 2 1

To Tom and Missy's
Easter Egg

Thanks to
Ingrid Beach
and Father Ted

CONTENTS

Easter: Prologue
1

Eostre
3

Passover/Pascha
6

The Date of Easter
8

The Other Dates of Easter
10

Easter Eggs
12

The Easter Bunny
15

Easter Music
17

Other Easter Customs
21

Florida and Easter Island
23

Lent
25

Shrove Tuesday and Mardi Gras
27

Ash Wednesday
30

Approaching Jerusalem
32

Palm Sunday
35

Monday in Jerusalem
36

Tuesday in Jerusalem
38

Wednesday in Jerusalem
40

Maundy Thursday—The Last Supper
42

Good Friday—The Crucifixion
44

Holy Saturday in Jerusalem
46

The First Easter
47

Easter: Prologue

Devoted to the resurrection of Jesus, the ultimate basis of Christianity, Easter was the first Christian festival. It predates even the celebration of the birth of Jesus, Christmas, and for centuries was the far more popular holiday. December 25 was set as the birthday of Jesus more than three centuries after his death, and religious scholars still don't agree about the exact day of Christ's birth. Very few people thought the birth special at the time, and it took place in a small country town, so the event wasn't very well documented. But the crucifixion of Jesus took place in Jerusalem, the capital city of Judaea, and was witnessed by a large number of people who had great interest in it. His death and resurrection then became the basis for a new religion by people who spread out across the world proclaiming its importance to all mankind. Small wonder that Easter, the celebration of Christ's death and return, has never lost its power to move and amaze us, and bring us back year after year to focus on our most sacred beliefs.

The celebration of Easter centers on Holy Week, the last days of Jesus's life on earth, and this week is observed with similar rites and rituals throughout all Christendom, by all branches of the faith. Beyond this, however, local customs have sprung up in every land. No book could chronicle all the different customs that Christians have observed every spring, so this book concentrates on the common customs of North America and the most interesting customs of other lands.

There are twenty-two chapters in this book, so you can start your reading on the Sunday that comes three weeks before Easter, and continue with one chapter per day until Easter Day. The last nine chapters tell the story of Jesus's final days on earth, and so are particularly good for counting down the Holy Week. But you can also read the chapters at any time—even in one sitting if you want. It's up to you.

To gain a greater understanding of all that Easter has become, we'll begin in the next chapter at the very beginning—with the ancient celebrations of the season, spring. These celebrations that predate Christianity will show us how spring and other rites and beliefs led to this most important of all Christian festivals.

Eostre

As far back as human history is known, people have celebrated the turning points of the year. In the Northern Hemisphere, the day with the least light comes about December 21 and is called the winter solstice. Thereafter, the sun begins to return from winter's darkness, and the amount of daylight grows greater each day. At the vernal (spring) equinox, falling somewhere around March 21, daylight and the dark of night become equal in length, and for the next six months, the days are longer than the nights. For that reason, ancient peoples, so dependent on good weather for growing their crops and raising their animals, celebrated spring. They knew they had survived the time of darkness.

Fires on hillsides to "encourage" the sun's return were traditional; it was believed that as far as the light shone the land would be fruitful. After these fires had burned, cattle were driven through the ashes and people jumped over the embers, all to bask in the joy and warmth of this symbol of the sun's growing light.

In Babylonia, long believed to be the cradle of civilization, the goddess of the spring was called Ishtar. She was identified with the planet Venus, which, because of its position in the solar system, either rises before the Sun in the morning or sets after it in the evening, so that the planet appears to love the light. Venus is the only celestial body other than the Sun and the moon which can be bright enough to cast shadows on the Earth, and the Babylonians felt this showed Ishtar's power.

As the Babylonian civilization spread, the fame of Ishtar grew as well. In Phoenecia, she became *Astarte;* in Greece, *Eostre* (related to the Greek word "Eos," dawn), and in Germany, *Ostara* (related to the German word "Ost," east, the direction of dawn). When this celebration of spring was combined with the specific celebration of Jesus's resurrection, it was not difficult to create the word "Easter" as a name for this holiday.

Many centuries later, when the Puritans came to North America, they regarded the celebration of Easter—and the celebration of Christmas—with suspicion. They knew that pagans had celebrated the return of spring long before Christians celebrated Easter, and they let that prejudice toward a pagan holiday blind them to the fact that the resurrection of Jesus was an actual event that should be celebrated. For the first two hundred years of European life in North America, only a few states, mostly in the South, paid much attention to Easter. It was not until the Civil War, when men moved away from their home states and mixed with others from all over, that local prejudices began to break down. But finally, it was the memorial services for the thousands of men who had fallen in battle and the Christian belief that with Christ's return all would live again that a greater appreciation of the day of resurrection began. Easter first became an American tradition in the 1870s. It was one way our country could ease its pain over the deaths of so many young men.

Passover/Pascha

    In addition to ancient festivals, another great religious festival takes place in spring—the night Jews call Passover.

    Passover first took place in the Jewish month of Nisan, some 1300 years before Jesus was born. On the Jewish calendar, which is based on the moon's cycles and is different from the modern calendar we use every day, each month begins with the new moon. The average time between new moons is a few days less than what we call a month on our calendar, which is keyed to the sun. Therefore, a Jewish year is shorter than the year we know from our standard calendar. Just as we have a leap day every four years to correct the imperfections in our calendar, the Jewish calendar has a leap month. So the Jewish months and holidays change from

year to year because of the lunar calendar, but the month of Nisan always falls near the spring equinox.

The Hebrews, or Jews, were slaves in Egypt at the time of the Passover, but Moses, one of their leaders, told them that God would bring tragedy to Egypt and force the Pharaoh to free them. Moses predicted a series of plagues, which came but did not move the Pharaoh to grant the Jews freedom. Still, the final plague from God would be the most terrifying. Moses commanded each Hebrew family to choose an unblemished lamb and slay it on the fourteenth of Nisan, which would be the night of the full moon. They were then to sprinkle the lamb's blood on the frame of the family's front door. Finally, the lamb was to be roasted and eaten with unleavened bread and bitter herbs by all family members.

That night, the Angel of God destroyed the firstborn children of the Egyptians but *passed over* the houses marked with lambs' blood by the Hebrews. The next day, the Egyptian Pharaoh released the Hebrews from slavery, ordering them to leave the country as quickly as possible. That leaving was called the Exodus, arguably the greatest event in Jewish history. Passover was decreed by Moses to be celebrated every year on that date for all time.

Thirteen hundred years later, Passover was still being observed, as Moses had commanded; Jesus, who was Jewish, was observing it during what we now call the Last Supper, which we'll learn more about later.

The date of Jesus's birth is uncertain and still debated by scholars, but Jesus's death took place on a most holy day of sacrifice, giving it incredible significance to Christians. The symbolism of the unblemished lamb, which must be killed to save others, was clear to everyone from the start. That is the reason the Gospel of John calls Jesus "the Lamb of God who takes away the sin of the world!"

The Date of Easter

Just as Christianity grew out of Judaism, Easter grew out of Passover. For that reason, there is no fixed date for Easter, because there is no fixed date for Passover on the non-Jewish calendar. This led to a number of problems that those who followed Jesus had to solve.

First, Passover can occur on any day of the week. But since Jesus was resurrected on a Sunday, the early church fathers became divided over whether to observe Easter always on a Sunday or let it move according to the date of Passover each year. The churches in Asia wanted Easter on Passover, citing the apostle John's observance of that tradition, while the churches in Europe and Africa argued for the Sunday which followed Passover. In time, both sides agreed to keep Easter always on a Sunday.

However, there is another problem in linking Easter to Passover. The Jewish calendar, based on moon cycles, has months that move compared to a calendar based on the sun. Because of this, Passover can occur before the spring equinox. But as we've seen, even two thousand years ago, the use of the equinox as the symbol of the sun's resurrection from the darkness of winter was already an old tradition, so many church leaders felt uncomfortable with a resurrection celebration falling before the equinox. These men argued that the first Easter had been tied to Passover, original-ly the first full moon after the equinox, and wanted to use that as the determining date, instead of the actual Passover date in any given year.

After much discussion, the majority of the early churchmen voted to establish Easter as *the first Sunday after the first full moon after the equinox.* But the Asian churches, unwilling to leave Passover out of the calculations, refused to agree. Late in the second century, Pope Victor excommunicated those churches, but they simply refused to recognize Victor or his successors as Pope and continued their traditions with their own leaders, becoming known as the Eastern Orthodox Church.

Still, there were two more problems. The first was astronom-ical: When is the equinox? It generally falls around March 21, but the Roman empire, still in existence and still very powerful, had officially decreed the equinox to be March 25.

The second was political: Since the full moon could, of course, fall on a Sunday, it was possible for Easter to actually occur on Passover. This meant that the European churches would have to celebrate at the same time as the Jews, and the early Christians were trying very hard to distinguish themselves from the Jews.

In AD 325, at the Council of Nicaea, the Pope's churches chose the 21st for the equinox, and added a second condition for choosing the date to observe Easter: *if the full moon falls on a Sun-day, Easter is the Sunday after.* This is the rule we in the West still follow today; Easter falls between March 22 and April 25.

The Other Dates of Easter

As we said before, the Eastern Orthodo[x] churches can celebrate Easter—which the[y] call Pascha*—at a different time from t[he] Western churches. The Eastern church h[as] agreed with the other early church fathe[rs] to set Pascha as the first Sunday after t[he] first full moon, but instead of counti[ng] from the equinox, they counted fro[m] Passover. Since the date of Passover diffe[rs] from year to year on our sun-oriented ca[l]endar, it could occur before the equino[x,] which worried the Western churches—b[ut] it could also occur up to four weeks *after* t[he] equinox, putting the Eastern Pascha [as] many as four weeks later than the Weste[rn] Easter.

And there was one final complication. [In] the early centuries of Christianity, wh[en] these questions were being decided, bo[th] Western and Eastern churches develop[ed] tables to calculate the date of Easter, based [on] the rules we've just explained. These tab[les] were supposed to help all priests of e[ach] denomination keep to the same date, even [if] they were not in contact with their cent[ral] authority, or had such bad late-win[ter] weather that they couldn't see the phases [of] the moon. Unfortunately, the early prie[sts'] astronomical knowledge was limited. By [the] 1500s, these tables had become significan[tly] inaccurate. The Western churches decid[ed]

*The Hebrew name for Passover is *Pesach*. The Greek [and] Latin use of it in relation to Easter changed it to *Pasc[ha,]* [the] name still used for Easter in many parts of the world.

to amend their tables and bring them back into alignment with the Sun and the Moon, but the Eastern churches again chose to keep to their traditions. The result is that today, the Eastern celebration of Pascha can occur up to *five weeks* after the Western Easter.

Meanwhile, the early churches in the far western part of Europe—specifically, the Celtic Christian churches of Ireland and Wales—developed their own doctrines concerning Easter. This was due not to differing traditions, but simply owed to the fact that the churches had very little contact with Rome before the Easter tables were devised; so these Celtic churches made their own calculations. Then, when communication with Rome was established fully in 597, these Celtic churches resisted changing their ways on orders from afar. It took more than seventy years before the question was "officially" settled, and even after that, battles were fought over the "correct" date of Easter for another hundred years.

Clearly, it is more difficult to celebrate Easter on earth than it is in heaven. But whatever the differences which have arisen among Christians around the world, it is, in the end, the belief and the celebration that counts.

Easter Eggs

And so, the celebration of Easter came into existence, focusing on the resurrection of Jesus but enhanced by many ancient traditions. Let's have a look at some of the most widely accepted enhancements, starting with Easter eggs.

As we'll see when we come to the discussion of Lent, eating eggs was once forbidden during the forty days leading up to Easter, so their long-untasted flavor came as a particular treat. But more than that, the wonder of newborn animals in the

spring obviously goes back to the earliest times, and a newly hatched chick fits the theme of Easter particularly well. Birth from an egg is different enough from the way humans and most other animals are born to stand out as something special. To some, breaking out of an egg recalls Jesus escaping his tomb.

The eggs of chickens are white or brown, but the eggs of wild birds are various colors, and have to be hunted for. As farming replaced hunting for most people, the old traditions were remembered by coloring chicken eggs at home, then hiding them for children to find (the first children's Easter baskets were just copies of the birds' newly-woven nests). Coloring of eggs was originally done with the new spring flowers. By arranging the flowers and their leaves around the eggs in pretty patterns, the image of the wrapping plants was left in white against the surrounding color, after the eggs were dipped in dyes made from other plants.

Often people tried to make one egg more elaborate than the last. This has been taken to its extreme in the elaborate Easter eggs which are still made by the people of the Ukraine. The Ukrainians melt wax and use it to draw on the egg, covering any area they want to remain white. The egg is placed in dye, coloring the unwaxed parts. The wax is applied again, covering any area that is to remain the just-dyed color. The eggs are then waxed and dipped in a new dye, and so on and so on...until a beautifully elaborate pattern appears.

These eggs inspired the Russian Czar to commission goldsmith Peter Carl Fabergé to create an ornate egg made of gold and jewels for the Czarina at Easter. For the next thirty-three Easters, until the Communist revolution of 1917 in Russia, Fabergé crafted increasingly elaborate eggs, all of which are still considered the ultimate in artifice. These eggs, which may be seen today in museums, are worth from three to five million dollars each.

Another tradition takes place in Germany, where fresh eggs are emptied out without breaking the shell, by poking a hole with a needle in both ends of the egg and carefully blowing the contents out. The empty eggshells are then decorated and hung from trees like Christmas ornaments. Today, many people decorate trees in their yards with brightly colored plastic eggs.

But being broken is still the fate of most Easter eggs, whether eaten or not. Many parts of the world have games where children roll eggs down a hill. The eggs bump into each other, with the last one to remain unbroken being the winner. The best-known version of this game takes place every year in Washington, D.C. at the White House, with the Presidential egg-rolling party. This party began as an impromptu sport on the slopes of the Capitol a few years before the Civil War, and now is a national event.

The Easter Bunny

Eggs symbolize a special form of birth, different from most other animals, but of those other animals, rabbits are best known for the size of their litters. So it is that rabbits also became a symbol of springtime and fertility in ancient days. Rabbits are not known for having little rabbits inside eggs, but once they were tied to the other customs of the time, the "Easter bunny" supposedly took on that ability.

The number of their babies is not the only connection rabbits

have to this time, though. Earlier, we talked about the difference between the calendar based on moon cycles and the calendar based on sun cycles. In ancient Egypt, the rabbit was a symbol of the moon god. Thoth, the Measurer, won from the rabbit the extra days which were necessary to change the lunar calendar to the solar calendar. The rabbit is a symbol of the moon for many cultures, from Native American to Chinese; though many people talk about the man in the moon, many others believe it's a rabbit up there.

Possibly tied to the same connection between the moon and the sun, a legend originated in the Middle Ages that the sun dances, or at least makes three cheerful hops, on Easter morning. To this day, some of the people around the world who gather for Easter sunrise services keep a careful eye on the dawning sun to see if it moves.*

Though the rabbit has thus been an accepted part of Easter for centuries, it is the one symbol of the season which has no official connection with Christianity. The only mention of rabbits in the Bible comes in the Old Testament, where Jews are commanded not to eat them; the Christian church has never recognized rabbits as having any significance at all.

On the other hand, the lamb, which plays only a very little part in Easter celebrations, has been considered the most holy animal of the season since the night of the original Passover. Meeting a lamb by accident during the Easter season is considered an omen of great good luck in the coming year, since the Devil can't assume the form of the animal ascribed to Jesus.

* Careful indeed, since no one should ever look directly at the sun for any length of time. Whenever you want to check the sun, poke a pinhole in a piece of cardboard and let the sun shine through the hole to form an image on a piece of paper.

Easter Music

The opera *Parsifal*, written by Richard Wagner in 1883, is presented around the world at Easter time, and a section of it called "The Good Friday Spell" is played even more frequently. The opera concerns an innocent fool (which is what "Parsifal" means) who finds the lance that pierced Christ's side as he hung on the cross, and the cup which caught Christ's blood; this cup

is the legendary Holy Grail. Through knowledge of these relics, Parsifal becomes, on Good Friday, the redeemer of his people.

Other musical compositions for this time include Johann Sebastian Bach's *Saint John Passion* and *Saint Matthew Passion,* George Friedrich Handel's *Messiah* (which was written for Easter but is now more often heard at Christmas), and Franz Joseph Haydn's *The Seven Last Words of Christ.* In addition to serving as Haydn's musical inspiration, these seven words—actually seven phrases—often form the basis for seven sermons during Lent, as each word is explored for its ultimate meaning. They are:

Father, forgive them; for they do not know what they do.
Luke 23:34

Woman, behold, your son!
John 19:26

Truly I say to you, today you shall be with Me in Paradise.
Luke 23:43

My God, My God, why hast Thou forsaken me?
Matthew 27:46

I am thirsty.
John 19:28

It is finished!
John 19:30

Father, into Thy hands I commit My Spirit.
Luke 23:46

In more recent times, popular secular songs such as "Here Comes Peter Cottontail" and Irving Berlin's "Easter Parade" have joined the Easter roster. The movie of the same name featuring Berlin's song and starring Fred Astaire and Judy Garland has become a perennial Eastertime television attraction.

Other Easter Customs

Because all that remained of Jesus on earth after the Resurrection was the linen he was buried in, early Christians took to wearing brand-new linen wraps on Easter. Because, in effect, Jesus took on "new clothes" when he ascended to Heaven, the early linen wraps evolved into new clothes for people. People believed this new clothing would bring good luck throughout the year.

The most well-known form of clothing was the Easter bonnet, a beautiful new hat festooned with ribbons and flowers of the season. Eventually, all this wearing of new clothing led to organized Easter parades, following the Easter Sunday church services. The most famous Easter parade in America is still held on Fifth Avenue in New York City.

The most famous flower of the season is the Easter Lily. This white spring flower with its velvety smooth texture, graceful length, and beautiful scent has been considered a symbol of purity since long before the time of Jesus. Nowadays, bouquets of these lilies are everywhere displayed in churches and homes at Eastertime. (There is also a so-called Lent Lily, but this is actually a narcissus.)

Possibly the most unusual custom associated with Easter occurs in Sweden, where, in addition to eggs and bunnies, the children celebrate with small dolls representing the Easter Witch! Though cute and funny nowadays, these dolls probably date back to the days when people believed that evil spirits haunted the darkness before Christ (or the sun) was reborn. That rebirth was and is said to frighten the witches away, so that they all flew up to a high mountain. While there, no doubt complaining about this turn of events, they were said to drink coffee, so the dolls always show the witches riding a broomstick with a coffee pot hanging from it. Interestingly, Sweden doesn't celebrate Halloween, but children dress up as Easter witches at Easter and go from house to house looking for gifts of candy!

Florida and
Easter Island

A day as significant as Easter has played a significant role in place-names around the world. The discovery of a "new land," especially by men sailing on vast, unknown oceans, clearly felt like a form of resurrection.

Finding palms for Palm Sunday has always been difficult in Europe, so other trees and even flowers have become part of the celebration. In Spain, the Easter Holy Week was known as *Pascua Florida*—Flowering Easter. When Ponce de León first sighted America's southern peninsula in 1513, it was Easter Day, so he called the land he saw "Florida."

Easter Island is a chunk of volcanic land 15 miles long and 11 miles wide, 2,000 miles west of Chile and 1,100 miles east of the next inhabited island. It was "discovered" by a Dutchman named Jacob Roggeveen on Easter Day, 1722, and he gave it an appropriate name. Several thousand people who called it *Rapa Nui* already lived there, of course, and their ancestors had carved strange, huge stone heads which amazed the Dutchman and everyone else who's beheld them since. The heads were cut from soft volcanic stone and ranged from 12 to 20 feet in height. They all had a distinctive elongated face with drooping ears; many had tall cylindrical hats (up to 6 feet) cut from a different sort of red stone.

The great heads sat atop burial platforms called *ahu*. These were sacred places honoring the native people's ancestors. Some 260 of these platforms were built, mostly along the coastline, though only 100 or so actually held heads. The platforms formed walls which ran parallel to the coastline; on those with heads, up to 15 once perched on the wall, all looking inland. But the Dutch crew and those who followed toppled the heads, so that none remain on the platforms today, and many are now shattered.

Lent

Lent comes from an Anglo-Saxon word, *Lengten*, meaning "lengthen," referring to the lengthening of the days after the winter solstice. The word was adopted by the early church in England as the name for the period leading up to Easter. As the time acquired a more specific character in the church, the word came to have the meaning we give it today: the forty days between Ash Wednesday and Easter. There are, in fact, forty-six days between the two, but the intervening Sundays, being special already, aren't counted.

Forty is a number which occurs several times in the Bible, always in the context of cutting oneself off from one's normal life. Noah's ark was built to survive a rain of forty days and forty nights. The Jews spent forty years wandering in the desert, Jesus spent forty days in the desert, Moses spent forty days on Mount Sinai, and Jesus spent forty hours in his tomb.

Fasting—another way of cutting oneself off from normal life by not eating—has long been a Lenten tradition. With the very first Christians, nothing at all could be eaten for the forty hours before Easter morning, beginning at 3 PM Friday, the time Christ died. In the early centuries of the Christian era, a less inclusive fast was extended back one week before Easter, then two. At the Council of Nicaea in 325, where so much of the doctrine concerning Easter was determined, a Lenten fast of forty days was discussed, but primarily as a preparation for baptism, and not as a general practice for all Christians. Around the year 600 Pope St. Gregory the Great ordered a specific fast to last the entire forty days: "We abstain from flesh meat and from all things that come from the flesh as milk, cheese, eggs, and butter." (Still, Sundays were exempt from the fast in the West; in the East, they were not.) This form of fasting lasted almost one thousand years, but then the strictures were loosened. Today, most Catholics require such fasting only on Ash Wednesday and Good Friday, while other Christian faiths no longer fast at all. But the Orthodox Eastern Church and the Eastern Catholic churches still hold to the traditional ways.

For primitive peoples, fasting in the spring was less a religious requirement than a practical one. These people harvested their crops in the fall, slaughtered the animals they expected to need for meat, and then had to survive until the spring with whatever they had. Naturally, by the end of the winter, the supplies were running low, and a freely accepted plan to cut back even further on eating helped the entire community.

Shrove Tuesday and Mardi Gras

Because there are forty (non-Sunday) days in Lent, the first Sunday in Lent traditionally commemorates the number by taking the name Quadragesima (fortieth). Also by tradition, if not mathematics, the Sunday just previous to Lent is called Quinquagesima (fiftieth), and the two before that are Sexagesima (sixtieth) and Septuagesima (seventieth). From Septuagesima Sunday, the word "Alleluia" ("Praise the Lord") stops being used in Catholic churches, not to be heard again until Easter Day.

When Pope St. Gregory decreed that Lent should have no meat, Quinquagesima Sunday, the final Sunday before Lent, came also to be known as Carnevala (farewell to meat), from which came the word "Carnival." Another preparation for Lent consisted of going to confession two days later, just before the period began on Ash Wednesday. This day of confession became known as Shrove Tuesday, because the confessed were forgiven (shriven) of their sins. But after confession, the people were faced with finishing off the nonmeat foods that couldn't be eaten—or even kept in the home—during Lent. Add that to the natural human urge to have "one last fling" before the hardships of the Lenten fast began, and the tradition of Carnival began. Stuffing oneself with rich delicacies became the norm on Shrove Tuesday, and it acquired the alternate name of Fat Tuesday—in French, Mardi Gras. These festivals are still celebrated today with wild, raucous parades, dancing, and people wearing elaborate costumes. The best known Mardi Gras/Carnival fes-

tivities take place in New Orleans and Rio de Janeiro, Brazil.

For many years in England, the country was famous for its Shrove Tuesday pancakes, which used up milk, butter, and eggs forbidden during Lent. The best known Lenten pastry is the hot-cross bun, a raisin cake with a white sugar cross drawn on top. This, again, comes from ancient pagan tradition—the baking and eating of cakes to celebrate spring. Unable to break newly Christianized peoples from their traditions, the priests simply took them over and Christianized them as well, by drawing crosses on the buns.

Ash Wednesday

The first day of Lent has been called Ash Wednesday since Pope Urban II so decreed in 1099. As the great Lenten fast begins, each of the faithful has his or her forehead marked with a cross made of ashes, the ashes having been obtained in the burning of the palm fronds from the previous year's Palm Sun-

day. Palm fronds are saved each year to bring good luck to the home. During the Palm Sunday service, the priest intones, "Remember, man, thou art dust, and to dust thou shalt return." Genesis 2:7 tells of God forming man from dust before He placed him in the Garden of Eden. Genesis 3:19 tells of God speaking the words the priests use when He decided to remove Adam and Eve from the Garden. Ash Wednesday is a reminder of God's love and His Power.

Ashes as a visible sign of sorrow date back, once again, to early Jewish tradition. When the Christian church continued the practice, it was especially tied to Shrove Tuesday and the Lenten fast; people who were marked with ashes then were said to be in "quarantine," another word derived from the Latin for "forty."

Because milk, eggs, and fat were forbidden during Lent, a tasty dough of flour, water, and salt was developed by Christians, as early as the fifth century. They rolled it out and, since it was food for a holy time, they folded it together in the shape of arms crossed in prayer. The Latin word for "little arms" was *bracellae*, which, in the German part of the Roman Empire, became *brezel* (in German, pronounced "bretzel") and so became known to us in time as "pretzel."

So now we have discussed all the events and objects that accumulated to form what we now know as Easter. But we should never forget, as the Puritans did, that those things accumulated around a specific event: the resurrection of Jesus. From this point on in this book, we will follow the last days of Jesus, as he made his way toward Jerusalem and Heaven.

We begin some weeks before his arrival in the Holy City, as he prepared for the sacrifice he was to make for all mankind, as the Lamb of God.

Approaching Jerusalem

Some weeks before he was to die, Jesus came to the small town of Bethany, about two miles outside Jerusalem, near the Mount of Olives. A man, Lazarus, had died there, and Jesus was prevailed upon by the man's sisters, Martha and Mary Magdalene, to use his well-known powers to try to raise him from the dead. He did raise Lazarus, and when word of the miracle spread, he was acclaimed throughout the region as the long-awaited Messiah—the divine king who would free Israel from Roman occupation as the Angel of God had freed the Israelites from Egypt at the time of the first Passover.

But the priests and the Pharisees, the most conservative of the Jews, were dead set against anyone who would challenge their authority. They met in secret and decided that Jesus would have to die. Even among themselves, they used an excuse— that the coming of a king for the Jews would bring down the wrath of the Romans upon them—but there was little doubt they were doing it to protect their own positions. Jesus heard of their plotting and decided to leave the area for a time.

The word of his miracles continued to spread, however, and as the time for Passover neared, Jews throughout the country made a pilgrimage to Jerusalem to await his coming. There had recently been a revolt against the Romans, and even though it had failed, people were ready for the promised Messiah.

On a Friday, one week before the day he would die, Jesus returned to Bethany, where he stayed with Mary Magdalene, Martha and Lazarus. The next day, Saturday, the Jews' holy day, the crowds poured out of Jerusalem and filled Bethany, trying to get him to perform miracles for them. And he did do miracles. But afterwards, with the cheers for his work still ringing in his ears, he took his disciples aside and told them that when he went into Jerusalem, the priests would condemn him to death. Moreover, they "will deliver Him to the Gentiles to mock and scourge and crucify, and on the third day He will be raised up."

Palm Sunday

On Sunday, Jesus and his disciples set out from Bethany to travel the two miles to Jerusalem. Jesus knew of the prophecy, written 550 years before by the priest Zechariah, that the king of Zion would come riding on a young donkey, so he told his disciples to take one from the village for him. They did, and spread cloths over the donkey's back for him to sit on. Then he rode down the main road to the city. The other pilgrims to Jerusalem lined both sides of the road and spread their own clothes in the dust before him. Others cut down palm branches with their bright springtime buds and spread them on the road. And all of them were crying out, "Blessed is he who comes in the name of the Lord!"

The Pharisees made their way out of the city and went to Jesus. They told him the people were making a spectacle of themselves. They demanded that he tell them to be quiet. But Jesus told the Pharisees to be quiet themselves, saying that nothing could hold back the joy of the day. So he arrived in Jerusalem to the cheers of the people, but also to the anger of the ruling order.

For the rest of the day he was mobbed by his followers, and at sundown he went back to Bethany to pass the night.

To this day, people celebrate Palm Sunday with a procession in church and the waving of palm fronds during the service.

Monday in Jerusalem

On Monday, Jesus returned to Jerusalem. Those who knew him were still singing his praises, but many others there had only heard the many rumors about him and were not convinced he was the Messiah. Those who were for him argued with those who were against him, and everyone waited to see what he would do now that he'd arrived. They didn't have long to wait.

He went to the Temple, which was supposed to be the main holy place, and confronted the businessmen who used it as their office. He threw them out into the street. Then he invited the blind and the crippled into the Temple, and he healed them. So once more he rallied the people to his side but infuriated the ruling classes who had had things their own way before he arrived. The priests of the Temple went to him again, and complained that the people were calling him the "Son of David," which, since David was Israel's greatest ruler, was like calling Jesus "king." But Jesus rejected their complaints, quoting, as he often did, one of David's psalms: "From the mouths of infants and nursing babes Thou hast established strength…to make the enemy and the revengeful cease."

The priests then asked why they should believe he

deserved this honor, and what sign he could show them to prove that he deserved it. He answered, "Destroy this temple, and in three days I will raise it up." The priests and his disciples understood that the "temple" referred to his body, as he had done while he was approaching Jerusalem. But the people thought he meant the actual temple building—a misunderstanding which would soon become critical.

Leaving the people cheering and the priests fuming, he left the Temple and Jerusalem itself, to spend the night in Bethany again. And that night the rulers of Jerusalem began to wonder how they could ever hope to destroy him, with his popularity at its highest point ever.

Tuesday in Jerusalem

On Tuesday, Jesus came back to Jerusalem. He returned to the Temple and began to teach the throngs who poured into the city at dawn to hear him—but things were somewhat changed. The priests and elders began to harass him, asking him again by what authority he presumed to teach. He refused to answer them directly. Then the Pharisees sent their disciples to ask him trick questions, to get him to say something offensive to the Roman rulers so that they could charge him with some crime, but he saw who they were and avoided their traps, as well. Then the Sadducees, another conservative group, questioned him, and met with no greater success. Faced with his ability to outmaneuver them, the elders then gave up on trying to trip him up before the people. But Jesus pressed his attack on them, telling the crowds who filled the Temple that they should reject the elders.

When his day of teaching was done, he went back outside the city and rested on the Mount of Olives. Four of his disciples came to him and asked when he would appear to the world as the Messiah. He told them it would be in the future, not now—but that in two days, the Passover would occur, "… and the Son of Man is to be delivered up for crucifixion." Reflecting on the massive outpouring of support from the people in Jerusalem, the disciples found that hard to believe—and yet, they did believe everything Jesus said. It was very confusing to them.

That evening, a woman came to him with a costly vial of perfume and anointed him. Some of the disciples were angry, thinking the perfume could have been sold to provide money for the poor, but Jesus excused her, saying the anointing was a traditional way to prepare his body for its burial.

And yet, the elders of Jerusalem had not yet acted to destroy him. So Judas, whom some say was his closest disciple, went to the priests and offered to betray him.

Wednesday in Jerusalem

On Wednesday, Jesus again returned to Jerusalem and taught, but beyond that, the Bible has little to say about this day. It seems clear, however, that by now, the crowds who had misunderstood him when he said he would destroy the Temple and raise it again in three days were beginning to become disenchanted with him. That's the only way to explain their anger toward him when he was offered up to their mercy two days later, on Friday. If they believed that his overthrowing the moneylenders on Monday was the "destruction," Wednesday would have been "the third day."

Also on this day, Judas must have continued his work of delivering Jesus to the authorities. This work has always been a puzzle. Most people, including some of the disciples, felt afterward that Judas was simply an evil man, recalling another psalm of David: "Even my close friend, in whom I trusted, who ate my bread, has lifted up his heel against me." The problem with this is that Jesus, who saw everything that was to happen to him beforehand, not only let him do his work, but, at the Last Supper, urged him to do it. Since Jesus had prophesied that the priests would condemn him to

40

death, and this would lead to his being revealed as the Messiah, perhaps Judas felt that someone needed to spur the priests into action, to help Jesus fulfill his destiny. The English author Thomas De Quincey and others feel that Judas wanted to force Jesus to use his messianic power and so save Israel. But no one will ever know what was in Judas's heart; all we know is the result.

On this day during Holy Week, Catholic churches and some Protestant churches celebrate the ritual of Tenebrae (Darkness). The ritual begins with the church lit by candles, which are extinguished one by one, until only one remains, representing Jesus as the light of the world. That lone candle is carried behind the altar to hide its light, or is simply extinguished, but after a period of darkness, the candle is returned or relit, to sig-nify that death is not the end.

Church services on the succeeding days follow the tone of the days as Jesus experienced them.

Maundy Thursday—
The Last Supper

The festival of Passover begins, as do all Jewish days, at sun-down. So, as Thursday afternoon wore on, the disciples asked Jesus where they would be celebrating the feast. He told them to go to the house of a certain man, often thought to be Joseph

of Arimathea, and prepare for the evening. And so, just after sundown, the thirteen of them sat at dinner and performed the traditional rites. But afterward, Jesus said, "Truly I say to you that one of you will betray Me. The Son of Man is to go, just as it is written of Him; but woe to that man by whom the Son of Man is betrayed!" Judas, taken aback, asked, "I, Rabbi?" And Jesus replied, "You have said it," adding, "What you do, do quickly." So Judas left the supper.

Then Jesus performed a new ritual, offering each of the disciples bread: "Take, eat; this is My body"—and wine: "This is My blood." Following this, they sang a hymn and left Jerusalem to pass the night on the Mount of Olives, in the Garden of Gethsemane.

As they settled into the spring night, Jesus knew that his hours of freedom were limited, and predicted that the disciples would abandon him, which they all denied they would do. Jesus may have been the Son of God, but he was a man, too, and as the hour of his capture approached, he was beginning to become afraid. He asked his disciples to wait for him as he walked by himself and wrestled with his fears. He prayed, saying, "Father, if Thou art willing, remove this cup from Me; yet not My will, but Thine be done."

At length, he conquered his fears—but when he looked back all the disciples had fallen asleep. He realized that everything he'd said was still unreal to them—and at that moment, Judas arrived with the priests' men. Jesus greeted him, saying, "Friend, do what you have come for," and Judas came forward to kiss him, showing his compatriots which man was Jesus. The disciples awoke and tried to protect their master, but Jesus told them to let him go, saying, "How then shall the Scriptures be fulfilled, that it must happen this way?" So the disciples left him and fled in fear for their own safety.

Jesus was taken to the priests and elders. There, the high priest Caiaphas conducted a religious trial and demanded to know who Jesus thought he was. "Are you the Messiah, the Son of God?"

And Jesus answered, "I am."

Caiaphas took this for blasphemy and decreed that Jesus should die.

Good Friday— The Crucifixion

Early Friday morning, the priests and elders took Jesus to Pontius Pilate, the Roman governor of Judea, and told Pilate they wanted Jesus put to death. Pilate was inclined to go along with the rulers of the people he had to control, but when he asked Jesus if he was King of the Jews, all Jesus would answer was, "You say." To all other questions he remained silent, and this left the governor with no excuse for ordering an execution. So he put it to the people surrounding his headquarters, offering them the chance to save either Jesus or a man named Barabbas, who had been part of a failed revolt some weeks before. As Pilate expected, the people turned on the man they had thought would liberate them but was now apparently a failure, and chose mercy for the rebel Barabbas—sentencing Jesus to death.

The Roman soldiers whipped Jesus, put a crown of thorns on his head, and beat it cruelly into his flesh. Then they forced him to carry his cross through the streets to Calvary, where public executions

44

were held. The normal method of execution was nailing the condemned man to a cross—crucifixion—and letting the shock kill him. Around nine in the morning, they crucified Jesus. Then the soldiers put a sign over his head: THIS IS JESUS THE NAZARENE, THE KING OF THE JEWS."

The soldiers, the priests, and the people continued their abuse of Jesus all morning. There were two robbers crucified beside him, and one of them even joined in. "Are you not the Messiah?" he jeered. "Save yourself and us!" But Jesus knew his destiny all too well, and answered, "Father, forgive them; for they do not know what they are doing." Then the other robber asked Jesus for his blessing, and Jesus replied, "Truly I say to you, today you shall be with Me in Paradise."

As the hours agonizingly passed, none of his disciples came to comfort or even see him, because they were afraid they'd be crucified with him. Only women came—his mother Mary, and Mary Magdalene, and others—to keep a silent vigil, and they were made to stay at a distance.

Around noon, clouds covered the sun and the day became dark.

Around three in the afternoon, Jesus cried out for the final time ... and died.

That evening, Joseph of Arimathea, a follower of Jesus and possibly the man at whose house the disciples had celebrated Passover, went to Pilate and asked to bury Jesus. This was unusual because Jewish days begin at sunset, which meant that the Sabbath of Saturday had already begun, and Jews were not supposed to work. But if Jewish law didn't concern Joseph, it didn't concern Pilate either, so he gave Joseph the body. Joseph, after wrapping it with burial herbs in a clean white cloth, laid it in a tomb he had cut into a huge rock. Then he had another huge stone rolled against the entrance to seal the tomb, and left ... as the women who had watched all day continued their somber vigil.

Holy saturday in Jerusalem

On Saturday, most people of Jerusalem undoubtedly felt that the story of Jesus was over. They passed the Sabbath thinking, either sorrowfully or scornfully, of what might have been if Jesus had been the promised Messiah.

But the priests and elders were far less satisfied. They had not forgotten the prediction Jesus had made on Monday, that he would rise again. It occurred to them that the disciples might return from their hiding place, steal the body, and then tell people Jesus had, in fact, arisen. So in the evening, when the Jewish Sabbath was completed and it was proper to do so, the elders went to Pilate and asked him to assign soldiers to watch the tomb. Pilate, probably very tired of hearing about Jesus from these priests, nevertheless agreed. He even had his soldiers put a seal on the tomb so it would be apparent if the stone were moved at all.

Then the city went to sleep…

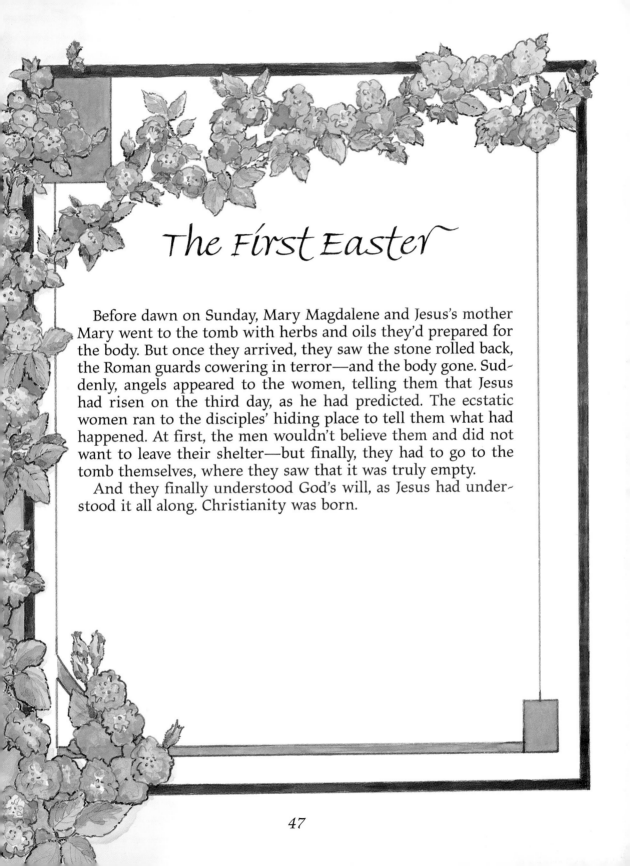

The First Easter

Before dawn on Sunday, Mary Magdalene and Jesus's mother Mary went to the tomb with herbs and oils they'd prepared for the body. But once they arrived, they saw the stone rolled back, the Roman guards cowering in terror—and the body gone. Suddenly, angels appeared to the women, telling them that Jesus had risen on the third day, as he had predicted. The ecstatic women ran to the disciples' hiding place to tell them what had happened. At first, the men wouldn't believe them and did not want to leave their shelter—but finally, they had to go to the tomb themselves, where they saw that it was truly empty.

And they finally understood God's will, as Jesus had understood it all along. Christianity was born.

Happy

Easter!